POLAR

WILDLIFE
AT THE
ENDS
OF THE
EARTH

Written by **L. E. CARMICHAEL**
Illustrated by **BYRON EGGENSCHWILER**

Kids Can Press

To my dad, for three years in Yellowknife that
sparked my enduring love of the North — L.E.C.

For Kelly — B.E.

ACKNOWLEDGMENTS

Thanks to the fabulous team at Kids Can Press and especially Katie Scott for
keeping me focused. Special thanks to the scientists who took the time to answer
my many questions. Biggest thanks to all the readers who want to know more
about amazing polar animals, both today and as the scientists of tomorrow.

Published in Canada and the U.S. by Kids Can Press Ltd.
25 Dockside Drive, Toronto, ON M5A 0B5

Kids Can Press is a Corus Entertainment Inc. company

www.kidscanpress.com

The artwork in this book was created digitally.
The text is set in Nalinak and Open Sans.

Edited by Katie Scott
Designed by Andrew Dupuis

Printed and bound in Shenzhen, China, in 10/2022 by Imago

CM 23 0 9 8 7 6 5 4 3 2 1

LIBRARY AND ARCHIVES CANADA CATALOGUING IN PUBLICATION

Title: Polar : wildlife at the ends of the Earth / written by L.E. Carmichael ;
illustrated by Byron Eggenschwiler.
Names: Carmichael, L. E. (Lindsey E.), author. | Eggenschwiler, Byron, illustrator.
Description: Includes index.
Identifiers: Canadiana 20220227209 | ISBN 9781525304576 (hardcover)
Subjects: LCSH: Animals — Polar regions — Juvenile literature. | LCSH: Animals — Adaptation —
Juvenile literature. | LCSH: Polar regions — Juvenile literature.
Classification: LCC QL104 .C37 2023 | DDC j591.70911 — dc23

Kids Can Press gratefully acknowledges that the land on which our office is located is the traditional
territory of many nations, including the Mississaugas of the Credit, the Anishnabeg, the Chippewa,
the Haudenosaunee and the Wendat peoples, and is now home to many diverse First Nations, Inuit
and Métis peoples.

We thank the Government of Ontario, through Ontario Creates; the Ontario Arts Council; the Canada
Council for the Arts; and the Government of Canada for supporting our publishing activity.

CONTENTS

Welcome to the Ends of the Earth 5

Where Are the Polar Regions? 6

A Warm Blanket 10

On the Move 12

Keeping Time 14

Ice-Cold Insects 16

Polar Seasons 18

Hide-and-Seek 20

Baby Food 22

In Sync 24

Cuddle Up! 26

A Long Winter's Sleep 28

Snowy Lands and Icy Seas 30

Speaking Up 32

Stride or Slide 34

Working Together 36

Fighting for the Future 38

Climate Change and the Polar Regions 42

How Polar Regions Affect Our World 44

Glossary 46

Resources 47

Index 48

WELCOME TO THE ENDS OF THE EARTH

Some of the harshest habitats on the planet are found in the polar regions. In the far north, the Arctic is an ocean surrounded by land. In the far south, Antarctica is a land surrounded by ocean.

The Arctic as we know it today emerged at the end of the Ice Age, approximately 12 000 years ago. Antarctica is much older, having existed in its current form for almost 20 million years. In summer, the Arctic gets warm enough for plants to grow, while almost all of Antarctica remains a frozen, barren landscape.

While different in many ways, the polar regions are also a lot alike. They are bitterly cold, freeze-dried wildernesses, where the wind can blow harder than hurricanes. They are also the only places on Earth where daylight — and darkness — lasts up to six months.

And yet many animals not only survive in the polar regions, they thrive. Over thousands — or even millions — of years, these species have adapted to the challenges of polar life. Animal adaptations include body parts, such as snowshoe paws, and body functions, such as making antifreeze. Or they may be behaviors such as migration, which some species use to escape deadly winters. Adaptations help polar animals stay warm, find food and raise their babies ... all in two of the most extreme environments on Earth.

WHERE ARE THE POLAR REGIONS?

ARCTIC

The Arctic surrounds the North Pole and can be defined in several ways. In this book, the Arctic refers to the tundra — a land-based habitat so cold and dry that trees can't grow. Cold oceans surrounding the tundra are considered part of the Arctic, too.

Arctic Circle	
Tundra	

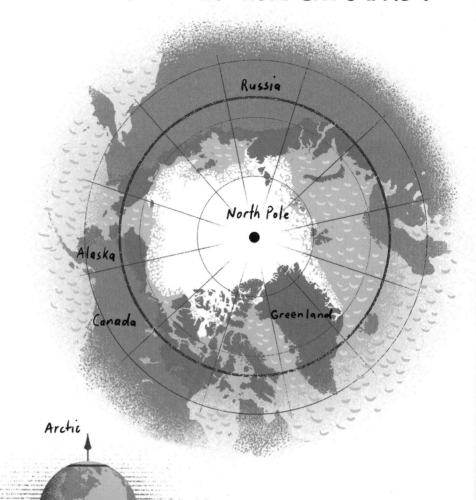

ANTARCTICA

Antarctica surrounds the South Pole and is defined by a current of moving water within the ocean. The Antarctic Circumpolar Current is the longest, strongest ocean current on the planet! This current encircles Antarctica, keeping the cold Southern Ocean isolated from warmer oceans to the north. It's the main reason Antarctic habitats have remained unchanged for millions of years.

	Antarctic Circle
	Antarctic Circumpolar Current

MIDNIGHT SUN AND POLAR NIGHT

The polar regions get different amounts of sunlight at different times of year. That's because the Earth is tilted on its axis as it orbits (travels around) the sun. In March, the Arctic tips toward the sun, causing sunrise at the North Pole. This begins a period of constant daylight called the midnight sun. In September, Antarctica tips toward the sun. As the midnight sun starts at the South Pole, the North Pole enters a period of constant darkness called polar night.

At the poles, the midnight sun and polar night last six months each. As you travel farther and farther away from the poles, these periods of continuous daylight and darkness get shorter and shorter. At the Arctic Circle and Antarctic Circle (imaginary lines encircling the top and bottom of the world), the midnight sun and polar night last just 24 hours each.

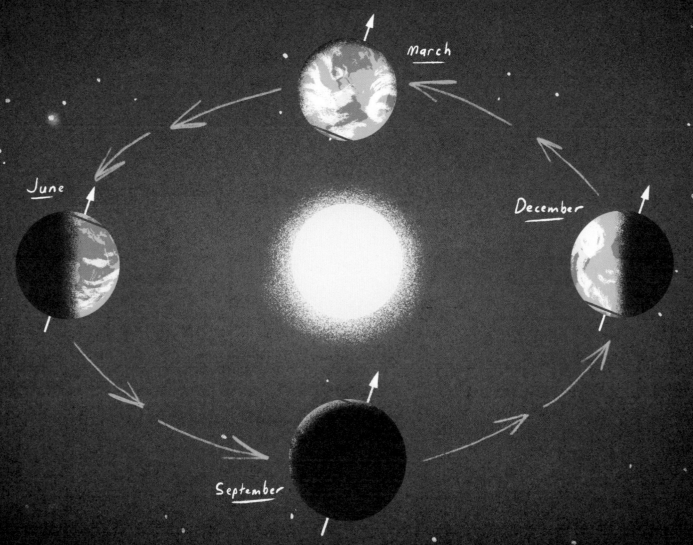

A WARM BLANKET

Staying warm in cold weather is a big challenge for polar animals. Warm-blooded mammals and birds make their own body heat but can freeze to death if that heat escapes their bodies. One solution is thick fur or feathers, an adaptation that helps prevent heat loss by trapping warm air against the animals' skin.

ARCTIC

MARCH. For weeks, the arctic fox has wandered, crisscrossing the frozen sea. Thick fur covers her toe pads, protecting them from the ice. No other type of fox has fur on the soles of its feet. No other type of fox could survive so close to the North Pole.

As the fox trots, wind ruffles her luxurious winter coat. It's twice as long as her summer fur, so she doesn't feel the cold. But hunger gnaws at the fox's stomach. If she can't find food, she won't survive much longer.

At last, she's crossed a polar bear's trail. If she follows him, perhaps she can steal his leftovers. Her luck isn't the only thing that's changing today. Overhead, the northern lights fade, giving way to a warm glow. Six months after it set, the sun peeks above the horizon once more. Dawn breaks, and the fox blinks.

Daylight has returned to the Arctic.

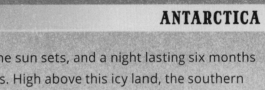

ANTARCTICA

MARCH. At the South Pole, the sun sets, and a night lasting six months begins. But all is not darkness. High above this icy land, the southern lights bloom. Streamers of light pulse and fade, dancing to the *pop-crackle-hiss* of their own music.

Wind surges in from the faraway coast. For an instant, the storm seems to hold its breath, and in the stillness between frigid blasts a south polar skua lands on the snow. The seabird is off course and exhausted from fighting the gusts. She must keep warm while she waits for calmer skies. Settling down, she draws her head into her chest, tucking bare legs beneath her belly. Her body warms the air that passes over her skin, and she fluffs her feathers, trapping that precious heat in a blanket of her own down. When the storm passes, she'll wing back home to the open sea.

ON THE MOVE

Certain animals migrate to different places as seasons change or at different times in their lives. Some visit polar regions in summer, hunting seasonal prey or avoiding predators that don't have polar adaptations. As winter approaches, these migrating animals escape to warmer regions closer to the equator. Other polar animals visit warmer regions only to find a mate.

ARCTIC

APRIL. The belugas spent the winter in the Bering Sea, between Russia and Alaska, where Arctic pack ice could not trap them. Now it's almost spring. The ice is melting, splitting, retreating toward the pole. The whales' migration route is opening up. The older females lead the way, north and east, teaching younger belugas how to find Canada's Beaufort Sea.

At more than 2500 km (1550 mi.), the belugas' journey takes months to complete. It's worth it. When the whales reach the Mackenzie River Delta, they'll rub against the ocean floor, shedding itchy layers of yellowed skin until they're glowing white again. Pregnant mothers will also give birth. The shallow coastal waters will protect the newborns from hungry orcas. While the babies play, their mothers will feast on krill and codfish, regaining their strength. Their rich milk will fatten the calves all summer, before the journey south begins.

ANTARCTICA

APRIL. The sperm whale was born in a warm tropical sea. At age six, he migrated to the cold Southern Ocean. For almost 20 years, he's roamed these deep waters — one of the few places on Earth with enough giant squid to satisfy his appetite. On this rich diet, he's grown big and strong, and longer than a city bus.

Stomach bursting after his latest hunt, the whale surfaces to breathe. A bitter wind is blowing, pancakes of ice sealing more of the sea every day. The whale's blubber is thick as a mattress, and he barely notices the wintry chill. Still, there's a reason to head for warmer waters: he's finally ready to find a mate. There are no female sperm whales in Antarctica. They spend all year in the tropics, feeding and protecting their young. So the whale turns north, away from the blossoming ice, and begins his first migration home.

KEEPING TIME

Animals have circadian rhythms: internal "clocks" that tell them the best time of day or night to eat, sleep or move throughout their habitats. In most parts of the world, these clocks are synchronized to daily cycles of light and dark. Polar animals, however, need flexible clocks to help them make the most of the midnight sun … or survive the polar night.

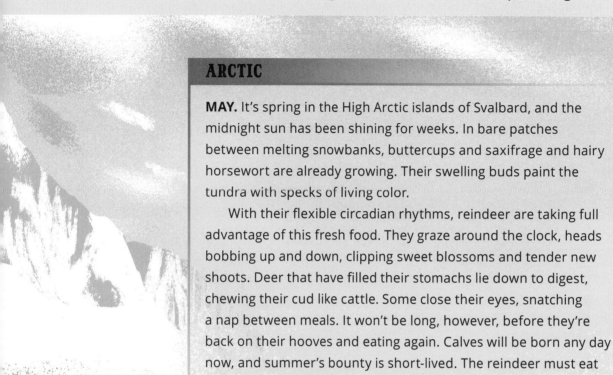

ARCTIC

MAY. It's spring in the High Arctic islands of Svalbard, and the midnight sun has been shining for weeks. In bare patches between melting snowbanks, buttercups and saxifrage and hairy horsewort are already growing. Their swelling buds paint the tundra with specks of living color.

With their flexible circadian rhythms, reindeer are taking full advantage of this fresh food. They graze around the clock, heads bobbing up and down, clipping sweet blossoms and tender new shoots. Deer that have filled their stomachs lie down to digest, chewing their cud like cattle. Some close their eyes, snatching a nap between meals. It won't be long, however, before they're back on their hooves and eating again. Calves will be born any day now, and summer's bounty is short-lived. The reindeer must eat all they can, fattening up before the sun sets and snow covers this tundra garden once more.

ANTARCTICA

MAY. Bransfield Strait, off the Antarctic Peninsula, is too far north to experience polar night. But winter's still coming, each day shorter and grayer than the last — especially when heavy snow clouds filter what's left of the afternoon light.

All summer, krill surfaced at sunset, eating floating algae when daytime predators couldn't see them. At dawn, they dove to feed on the seabed, hiding from hunters in the darker, deeper water. But as the seasons shifted, the krill's internal clocks lost control. Now, their daily movements are only loosely linked to the sun's rise and fall. Instead, krill respond to the brightness of the light, no matter where it comes from.

Today's sun has set, the light faded. The swarm of krill begins to ascend. But the storm clouds break just as the full moon is rising. In the sudden glare, these "werewolf plankton" flinch and pause, waiting for darkness to continue their journey in safety.

ICE-COLD INSECTS

Insects are cold-blooded: their body temperatures match the temperatures of their chosen habitats. In summer, insects warm up or cool down by moving between sunlight and shade. In winter, sheltered habitats help insects avoid the worst of the deadly cold. A second adaptation, protective antifreezes, keeps some insects alive even when the water in their bodies turns to ice!

ARCTIC

JUNE. Across the Arctic, snow is melting. The midnight sun warms islands of dark rock, which radiate heat into shrinking snowdrifts. At last, fingers of light stroke the soil at a boulder's base, warming a silken cocoon. The woolly bear caterpillar breaks free of her winter wrapper. She's got just 19 days to eat and grow before finding a new place to wait out the coming cold. She'd better get busy.

On the bare, damp earth, the caterpillar turns lengthwise to the sun, catching as much heat as she can. When she's warmed to 30.5°C (87°F), she moves, crawling toward the shade of an arctic willow. Her tiny jaws tear into the shrub's new leaves. But she's cooling down quickly and needs to bask in the sun again. The woolly bear caterpillar crawls back into the warmth, tracking the light like a sundial as it moves across the greening tundra.

JUNE. Snowflakes swirl and curl, dancing in the polar night. The storm clouds part, long enough for moonbeams to waltz across the drifts. Though all seems deserted now, in summer this island was a hive of movement. Under mounds of emerald moss, flightless midges swarmed in frantic mating frenzies. These insects, smaller than grains of rice, are Antarctica's largest land animals. They produce even tinier larvae. Under the midnight sun, those larvae writhed and wriggled, growing and eating and growing again.

Early frosts warned the larvae of the coming cold. They produced antifreezes, preparing themselves for winter. With these chemicals, the larvae can't *stop* from freezing, but they can *survive* freezing — especially if they find shelter. Tangled larvae lie beneath a pillow of moss and a blanket of snow. The water in their bodies has turned to ice, but they're still alive. When spring arrives, they will wake from their winter comas to dance again.

POLAR SEASONS

In most places, *summer* means long days and warm weather. In the polar regions, however, long days arrive sooner than warmth. One reason for this delay is that light-colored snow and ice reflect up to 90 percent of the sunlight that touches them. Because of their high albedo (a measurement of how much sunlight a surface reflects), snow and ice melt slowly ... and the weather doesn't change much until melting is done. Even once the ground has thawed, plants need time to start growing again.

Plants, rocks and soil are darker than snow and ice, so they have lower albedos. So do deep oceans, which absorb 90 to 95 percent of the sunlight that touches them. These dark surfaces store the sun's heat during summer and release it in autumn. Because of this stored heat, days get shorter before cold winter weather arrives.

SEASON	ARCTIC	ANTARCTICA
Spring	March to May	September to November
Summer	June to August	December to February
Autumn	September to November	March to May
Winter	December to February	June to August
Plant Growth	May to August	December to March
Warmest Month	July	January
Coldest Month	February	August

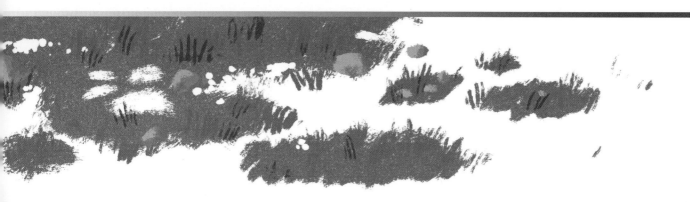

WILD WINTERS

Which polar region has the harshest winters? It depends on how you measure. The coldest temperature ever recorded on Earth, -89°C (-128°F), occurred in Antarctica. At -50°C (-58°F), exposed human skin freezes in less than two minutes! Antarctica also has the world's fastest winds, up to 327 km/h (203 m.p.h.). The fastest wind measured in the Arctic was only 252 km/hr (157 m.p.h.), but still equal to the most extreme hurricanes.

The Arctic gets more snow: up to 140 cm (55 in.) each year, the height of an average nine-year-old. In contrast, yearly snowfall in Antarctica is about 13 cm (5 in.), barely enough to trickle over the top of a snow boot.

No matter how you measure, one thing's for sure: polar winters are pretty wild!

CHASING SUMMER

For arctic terns, summer lasts all year. That's because these birds migrate between the Arctic and Antarctica, following long days and warm weather from one end of the globe to the other. It's a round trip of up to 50 000 km (31 068 mi.), the longest migration of any animal in the world. This extreme adaptation ensures that arctic terns are always in the right place, at the right time, to feast on seasonal prey.

HIDE-AND-SEEK

There are times to stand out in a crowd and times to blend into the background. For example, animals must be visible and attractive to potential mates, but they also must camouflage themselves from hungry predators. Unique adaptations, involving both body parts and behaviors, help some polar species strike the right balance between hide and seek.

ARCTIC

JULY. It's midsummer. Ponds of melted snow dot the tundra, reflecting blue like cups full of sky. Female ptarmigan have traded their white winter feathers for ones with brown speckles. Against bare ground, the birds almost disappear, invisible to hungry foxes and falcons. But male ptarmigan still *want* to be seen ... by potential mates. White feathers sparkling, they compete for the females' attention, fanning their tails and calling, *Wuk, wuk, wuk.*

One male has already found a match. While his mate lays their eggs, he must think of his own safety. The ptarmigan crouches in a mud puddle, beating his wings, flinging the filth with his beak. As he bathes, his bright feathers turn dull and dirty. A shadow passes overhead, and the ptarmigan freezes. Is that a gyrfalcon flying above? The predator circles but cannot see through the ptarmigan's camouflage. Clean white males, still visible from miles away, won't be so lucky.

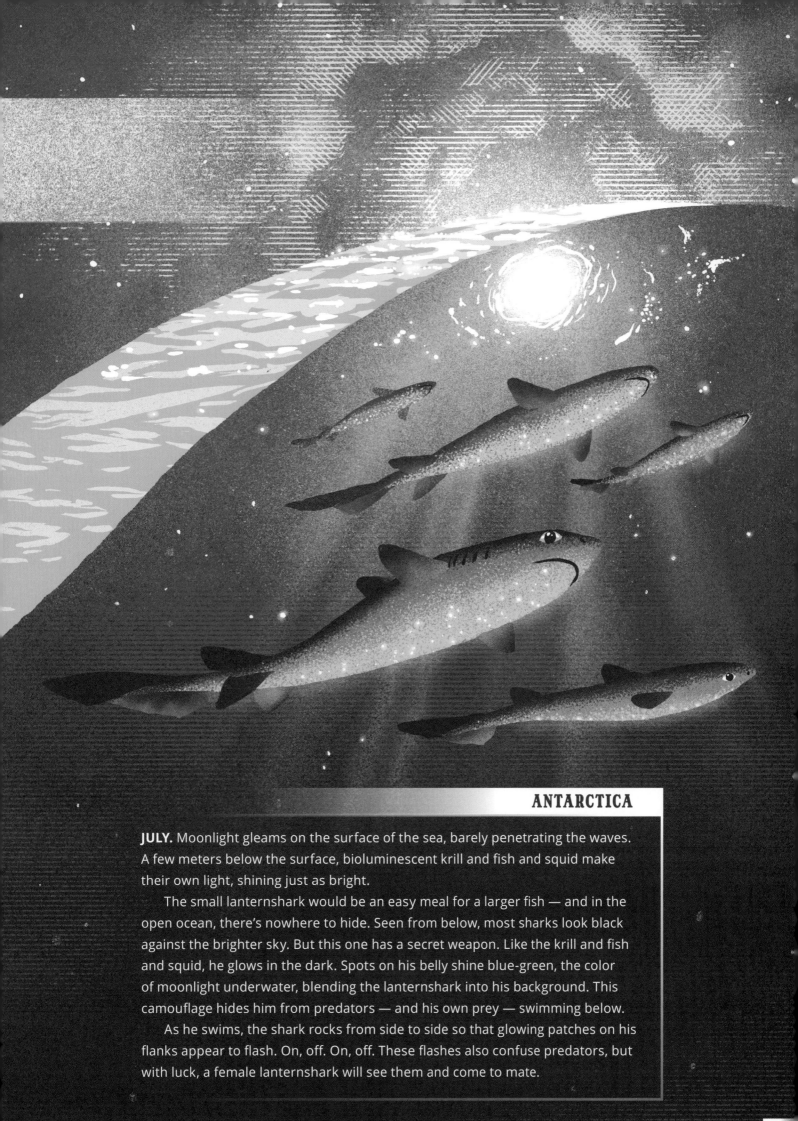

ANTARCTICA

JULY. Moonlight gleams on the surface of the sea, barely penetrating the waves. A few meters below the surface, bioluminescent krill and fish and squid make their own light, shining just as bright.

The small lanternshark would be an easy meal for a larger fish — and in the open ocean, there's nowhere to hide. Seen from below, most sharks look black against the brighter sky. But this one has a secret weapon. Like the krill and fish and squid, he glows in the dark. Spots on his belly shine blue-green, the color of moonlight underwater, blending the lanternshark into his background. This camouflage hides him from predators — and his own prey — swimming below.

As he swims, the shark rocks from side to side so that glowing patches on his flanks appear to flash. On, off. On, off. These flashes also confuse predators, but with luck, a female lanternshark will see them and come to mate.

BABY FOOD

Some polar babies fend for themselves just days or weeks after birth. To quickly grow their bodies and brains, the young need high-energy foods. Birds give nestlings plump, juicy insects, while mammal mothers make rich, ultra-high-fat milk. This nutritional jump-start helps young animals survive life at the ends of the Earth.

ARCTIC

AUGUST. In the afternoon light, fuzzy cotton-grass blossoms twinkle like fallen stars. A snow bunting searches for food on the nearby beach. The bird has stuffed himself with saxifrage seeds, but his nestlings need something more nutritious. When they hatched, each chick weighed about as much as three raisins. Ten days later, they're 10 times as heavy but still too small to migrate this autumn.

Luckily, this beach is speckled with ponds where insects swarm. The bunting snatches a caterpillar and wings back to his nest, tucked deep within a crack in a boulder. The chicks' hungry shrieks echo off the rock, deafening in this small space. The bunting drops his caterpillar into one gaping mouth, but others remain empty. He runs for the exit as his mate returns, a fly in her beak. Until the chicks are ready to leave the nest, both parents will feed them around the clock.

AUGUST. Southeast of New Zealand, in the ice-covered Ross Sea, a young Weddell seal arrows for the depths. Bubbles stream from her nostrils. The silverfish are a long way down, and she has to reach them before she runs out of air.

The seal has trained for this since her birth on the ice last November. On her mother's rich milk, she gained 2 kg (4.4 lb.) per day, about the weight of a soda bottle. Her growing muscles held more oxygen, increasing the time she could wait between breaths. Her brain grew, too, and the seal quickly learned how to find her way underwater. Since her first swim, at 10 days old, she's gained the knowledge and experience to survive on her own.

Now, as she darts through the school of fish, the seal's lungs burn with the need to breathe. One quick bite, and she shoots for the surface, and her favorite hole in the ice.

IN SYNC

In breeding season, many polar bird species live in large groups called colonies. Birds in each colony synchronize nest building, egg laying, and raising and fledging their chicks. This lets birds take advantage of baby foods or nest sites that are only available for a short time. Although birds in a colony sometimes compete for resources, they also protect each other from predators.

ARCTIC

SEPTEMBER. Every day since the horned puffin hatched has been the same: adult birds ebbing and flowing from the colony, leaving to fish, returning with food. After six weeks, the young puffin is almost as big as her parents. The last tufts of baby down cling to her new feathers. And something about today feels … different.

Carefully, alert for hungry gulls, the chick peers from her burrow. The sun hangs low, kissing the sea, and the chick feels something calling. She's not alone. Other chicks poke their heads out of crannies in the cliff, measuring the distance to the water.

All at once, young puffins are running, jumping, swooping, flapping. Gulls screech and wheel, trying to catch them, confused by the flurry of potential targets. In the relative safety of the crowd, the chick runs for it, tottering down the beach. When her toes touch water, she splashes, dives and swims into the sunset.

ANTARCTICA

SEPTEMBER. Sun rises over a colony of Adélie penguins, the smallest penguins in Antarctica. Males are arriving in hordes, hundreds more each day. As nest sites emerge along the melting coastline, the colony hums and buzzes and chirps and squawks with birds competing for space. The best spots are in the center of the honeycomb-shaped colony, where adults can band together to protect chicks from snatching skuas.

Location isn't everything. To win a female's heart, male Adélies need stones: a platform of pebbles to lift their eggs above icy spring floods. But with so many penguins building nests at once, there aren't enough stones to go around.

One male dips his head, stealing a pebble from another's nest. The offended penguin flipper-bashes the thief. In the ruckus, two other males swoop in, pecking each other before escaping with plunder of their own. The females will arrive any day now, and every male is desperate to impress.

CUDDLE UP!

Staying warm can be a challenge for small animals. That's because body heat escapes through the skin, and small animals have a lot of skin compared to their insides, whereas large animals have less skin compared to their insides. Some small creatures solve this problem with a clever adaptation — they cuddle! The huddle stays warmer than one small animal could on its own.

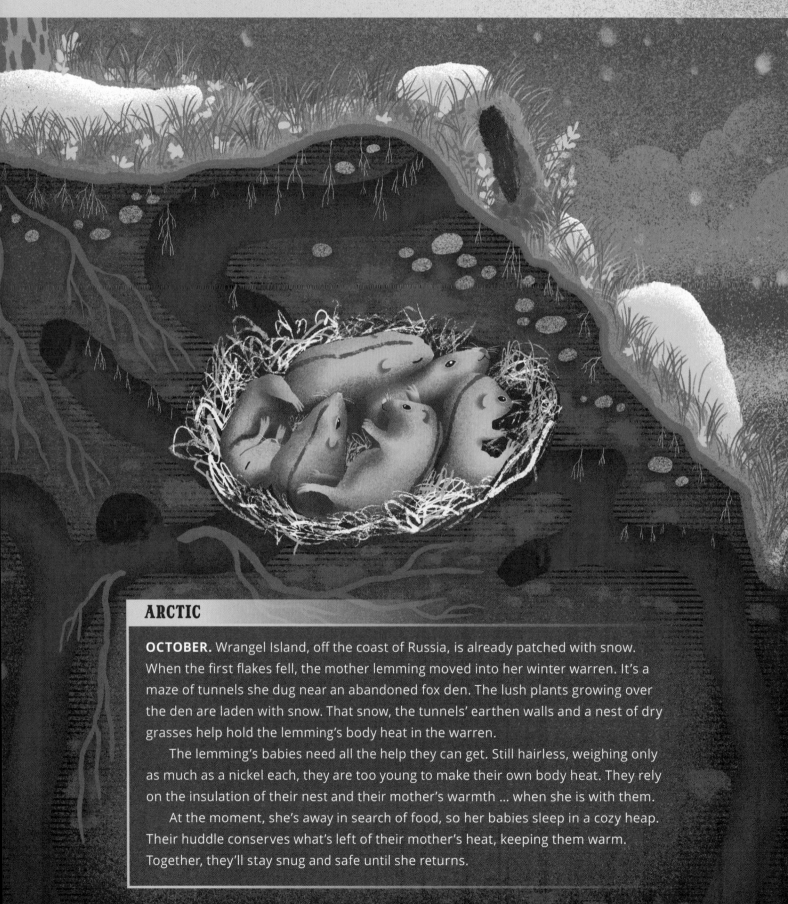

ARCTIC

OCTOBER. Wrangel Island, off the coast of Russia, is already patched with snow. When the first flakes fell, the mother lemming moved into her winter warren. It's a maze of tunnels she dug near an abandoned fox den. The lush plants growing over the den are laden with snow. That snow, the tunnels' earthen walls and a nest of dry grasses help hold the lemming's body heat in the warren.

The lemming's babies need all the help they can get. Still hairless, weighing only as much as a nickel each, they are too young to make their own body heat. They rely on the insulation of their nest and their mother's warmth ... when she is with them.

At the moment, she's away in search of food, so her babies sleep in a cozy heap. Their huddle conserves what's left of their mother's heat, keeping them warm. Together, they'll stay snug and safe until she returns.

OCTOBER. In autumn, thousands of emperor penguins left the open ocean, migrating onto the sea ice to breed. Through blackness and blizzards, males balanced eggs atop their feet, incubating them under a cape of belly feathers. Now it's spring. Other birds, in other colonies, are just beginning to breed. Here, parents fetch fish to feed their downy chicks.

But winter's chill lingers, and chicks are still building their insulating body fat. So the penguins huddle, sharing the work of staying warm. Flippers folded, beaks tucked between each other's shoulders, they circulate in tiny, synchronized steps. Chicks cluster at the hub of the wheel, and around the rim, adults take turns breaking the bitter wind.

Then one bird, and another, walks away. In minutes, a huddle that lasted hours disintegrates, releasing a haze of heat. Penguins drink, scooping snow into their beaks. As birds cool, new huddles come together across the ice.

A LONG WINTER'S SLEEP

Unlike a bear's shallow winter naps, true hibernation is a deep sleep in which body functions slow or even stop. This saves energy in winter, when food — an animal's energy source — is often scarce. Despite its benefits, this adaptation is rare in the polar regions. In the Arctic, only ground squirrels hibernate; Antarctica's black rock cod is the only hibernating fish in the world.

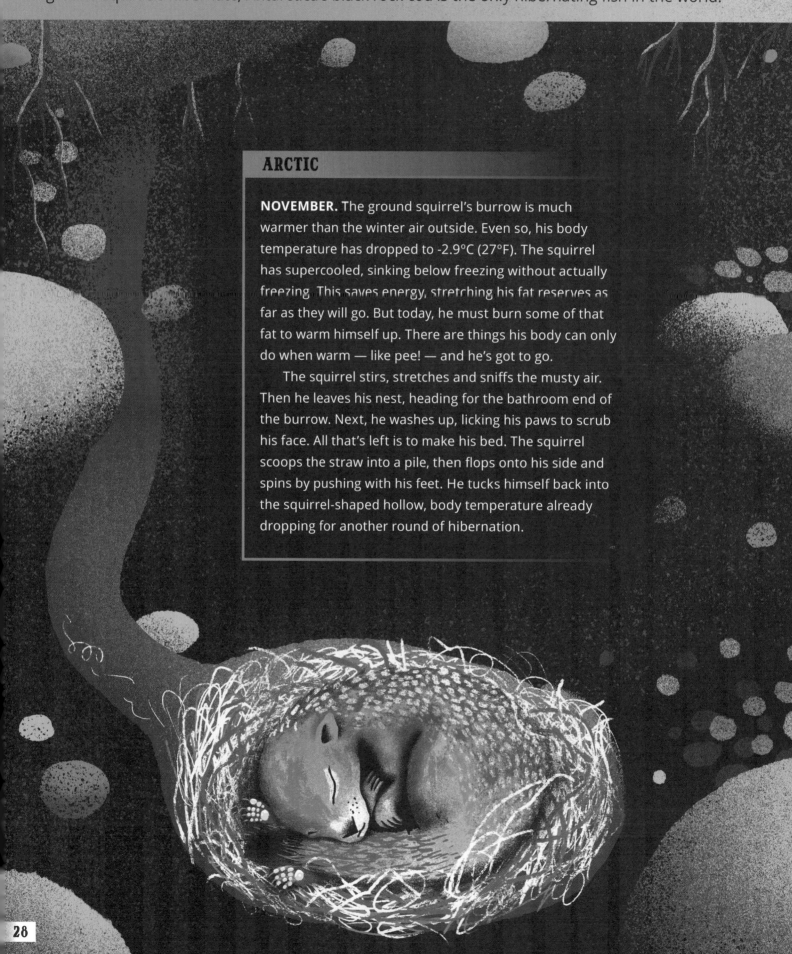

ARCTIC

NOVEMBER. The ground squirrel's burrow is much warmer than the winter air outside. Even so, his body temperature has dropped to -2.9°C (27°F). The squirrel has supercooled, sinking below freezing without actually freezing. This saves energy, stretching his fat reserves as far as they will go. But today, he must burn some of that fat to warm himself up. There are things his body can only do when warm — like pee! — and he's got to go.

The squirrel stirs, stretches and sniffs the musty air. Then he leaves his nest, heading for the bathroom end of the burrow. Next, he washes up, licking his paws to scrub his face. All that's left is to make his bed. The squirrel scoops the straw into a pile, then flops onto his side and spins by pushing with his feet. He tucks himself back into the squirrel-shaped hollow, body temperature already dropping for another round of hibernation.

NOVEMBER. Under the water, a rock cod slumps in a crevice between boulders. Through the long winter's night, while other fish fed and swam, the cod hibernated. She ate nothing, even when her favorite shrimp strayed right past her mouth. Instead, she conserved energy, hardly moving for up to 12 days in a row. She roused just long enough to find a new hiding spot before sinking back into sleep.

Now spring has come to the Southern Ocean. The water has warmed, the sea ice thinned. Streamers of sunlight dapple the seabed. The cod twitches, stirs. Her heart rate begins to rise, and she wants food for the first time in months. Cautiously — she's still too sluggish to escape a hungry leopard seal — the cod emerges from her hollow. She nibbles at the seaweed, swishes her tail fin and slowly swims away.

SNOWY LANDS AND ICY SEAS

On land or sea, snow and ice are major parts of polar habitats. Some animals migrate to avoid these conditions. Others have adapted to year-round life in the polar regions, coping with the challenges — and taking advantage of the opportunities — that snow and ice can bring.

Permafrost is earth that's been frozen for at least two years. It's found on land and underwater, in lake and ocean beds. Most plants can't grow in frozen soil, so permafrost affects which plants, and plant-eating animals, can live in polar regions.

In winter, the space under the snow offers warmth and protection for small animals, such as ermines and lemmings. Snow patches are valuable in summer, too, as a source of fresh drinking water. And predators, such as wolverines, store excess meat in snow to keep it from spoiling in the summer sun.

Glaciers are made of centuries-old snow that's turned to ice. Against a glacier's white background, wind-blown insects are easy for hungry birds to see.

Icebergs are large chunks of ice that break off of glaciers and drift into the ocean. Birds rest on them, and some, such as ivory gulls, even build nests on icebergs to avoid land-bound predators!

Sea ice plays an important part in polar food webs. When seawater freezes on the surface, the water below becomes extra salty and extra heavy. That water sinks, pushing up nutrient-rich water from the ocean floor. Algae use these nutrients to grow, becoming food for krill, which in turn become food for fish, birds, seals and whales.

Leads are cracks that form when wind and waves break apart sheets of sea ice. They provide breathing holes for whales and seals.

SPEAKING UP

During polar night, in deep dark water or at crowded breeding colonies, sound can be more important than sight. Some marine mammals use sounds to find prey or danger around them — a specialized adaptation called echolocation. Another adaptation is the unique calls animals use to find and identify their young after spending time apart.

ARCTIC

DECEMBER. All summer, the narwhal, her newborn and their pod sheltered in shallow coves off Canada's Arctic islands. The coves protected them from orcas, but there was no halibut in sight for the hungry mother. Now it's winter, and the pod has returned to ice-covered Baffin Bay, between Canada and Greenland. The mother dives into the inky ocean, deep as the Grand Canyon. Emitting a burst of sound, she scans the seabed for fish. The noise bounces off a large halibut, leading her straight to her favorite prey.

Full — for now — the narwhal swims for the surface. Another burst of echolocation guides her to a crack in the ice where she can breathe. She finds it crammed with other narwhals. Her calf, too small to dive with her, has been waiting somewhere in the crowd. The mother whistles, and her newborn's familiar call echoes back.

Reunited with her baby, the narwhal rests while nursing. This far from open water, they're safe from orcas. And today, neither of them will go hungry.

ANTARCTICA

DECEMBER. The fur seal pup is two weeks old and hasn't seen his mother in days. She's been away eating krill, which gives her energy to make his milk. The pup waits, tiny and fragile, on a dangerous beach packed with four million seals. He's surrounded by bellowing males and snarling females with pups of their own to feed.

A tussle breaks out. The little pup flees from being trampled and crushed. He's 10 m (11 yd.) away from where he was born, and his mother might have trouble finding him. Her eyes, adapted for underwater vision, see poorly in dry air. And she can't smell him unless they're close enough to touch.

Then the pup hears a low call. A dozen other pups look up — at this distance, the seal could be anyone's mother. But she keeps calling as she approaches, voice getting clearer, and the other pups turn away. She's no one's mom but his.

STRIDE OR SLIDE

Moving across the surface of the snow is faster — and uses less energy — than sinking in and breaking paths through the drifts. Animals that can do this have found ways to spread their weight over the largest possible area. Broad paws like snowshoes are one helpful adaptation. Tummy tobogganing is another!

ARCTIC

JANUARY. The blizzard lasted hours, covering the mountain's crown with a cap of fresh powder. Now the wind has died, and the slopes glisten in the moonlight. It's time to hunt. The Eurasian lynx yawns and stretches. Shaking snow from his thick, dense coat, he strides across the tundra. The drifts are deep, but his wide webbed paws, like snowshoes, barely make a dent.

The lynx sniffs at the holes where reindeer — heavy animals with narrow hooves — have fallen through the snowpack. He follows their trail, then stiffens. There's a hare in the shelter of a large rock, nibbling on a willow bush. The lynx crouches, his gaze intent, and stalks forward. His tail wriggles as he measures the distance. *Pounce!* But the hare's big back feet spread her weight even better than his do, and she skims away across the snow, faster than he can follow. He'll have to look elsewhere for tonight's meal.

ANTARCTICA

JANUARY. Chinstrap penguins come and go, bustling about the colony, feeding their screaming chicks. The mother chinstrap is hungry, too. She guarded her hatchlings while her mate was out at sea. Now that he's back, it's her turn to go feed. But before she can eat the krill, she has to get to them.

The colony is uphill from the ocean, above a rocky slope that's still covered in snow. The chinstrap waddles to the edge, each small foot sinking into the slush. Pulling them free takes too much of her waning energy. There's only one solution — tobogganing! The chinstrap flops, spreading her weight across her broad belly. She's not sinking anymore, she's sliding down the slope. Paddling with feet and flippers, she picks up speed, zipping to the shore. Then she dives, sailing through the water, snapping up the krill she craves.

WORKING TOGETHER

Animals of the same species often survive by working together. But cooperation between different species is rare, maybe because communication is tricky when animals speak different languages! Partnership between different species is called mutualism. In the polar regions, mutualism helps some animals find food and protect one another from predators.

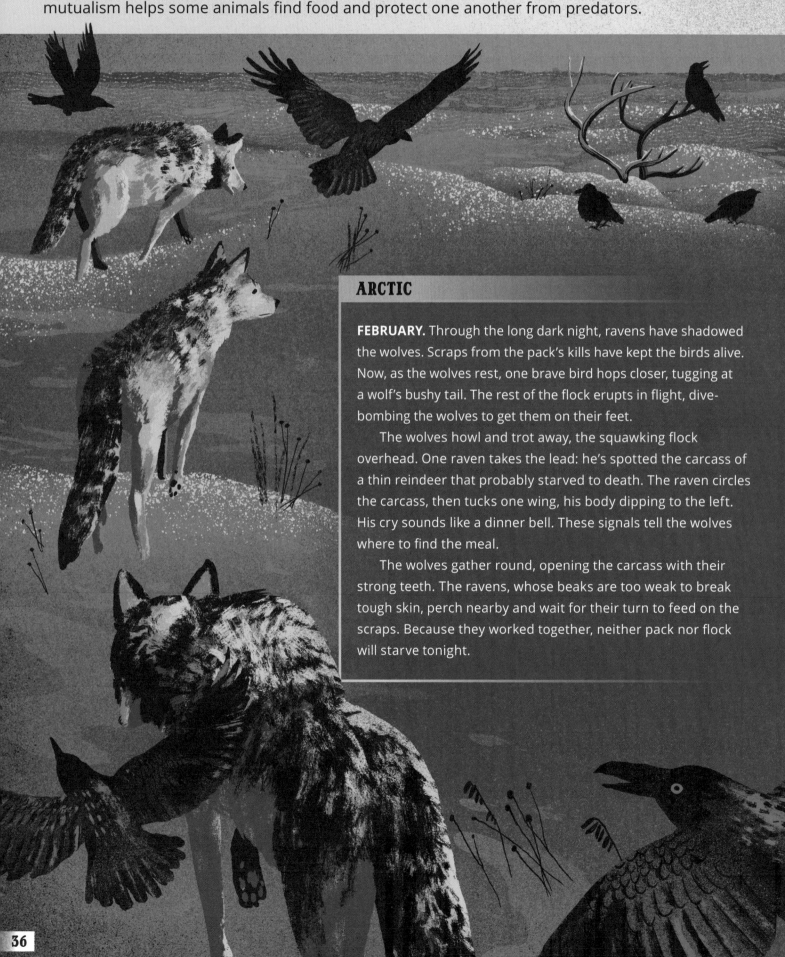

ARCTIC

FEBRUARY. Through the long dark night, ravens have shadowed the wolves. Scraps from the pack's kills have kept the birds alive. Now, as the wolves rest, one brave bird hops closer, tugging at a wolf's bushy tail. The rest of the flock erupts in flight, dive-bombing the wolves to get them on their feet.

The wolves howl and trot away, the squawking flock overhead. One raven takes the lead: he's spotted the carcass of a thin reindeer that probably starved to death. The raven circles the carcass, then tucks one wing, his body dipping to the left. His cry sounds like a dinner bell. These signals tell the wolves where to find the meal.

The wolves gather round, opening the carcass with their strong teeth. The ravens, whose beaks are too weak to break tough skin, perch nearby and wait for their turn to feed on the scraps. Because they worked together, neither pack nor flock will starve tonight.

ANTARCTICA

FEBRUARY. Algae have bloomed under the midnight sun, turning the sea a bright garden green. Krill have been feeding on these tiny plants. When eaten, the algae release a scent, like a chemical cry for help.

Miles away, across the barren ocean, seabirds smell the plants' distress signal. Prions and petrels follow it, flocking to the watery garden. They swoop and splash and snap up krill. The air vibrates with their squawks and shrieks.

Between meals, the seabirds rest on the rocking waves. The krill they've devoured are rich in iron, which will kill the birds if it stays in their bodies. So they poop it out! Those smelly bird droppings give algae an essential nutrient — iron — that's hard to find in seawater. The iron will help the algae grow, the krill will feed on the algae, and the seabirds will feast on the krill, continuing the cycle all summer long.

FIGHTING FOR THE FUTURE

In the polar regions, survival is about more than staying warm and finding food: it's about protecting the young. Young animals are the most vulnerable to predators, and if too many are lost, the species will dwindle … or go extinct. Adaptations that protect this next generation help the entire species to survive.

ARCTIC

MARCH. Musk oxen meander down the frozen river valley, pawing at the snow to uncover last summer's plants. It's been a long winter, and their stomachs grumble.

The grizzly bear is hungry, too. He's just emerged from his den, and he'll risk injury for a chance at fresh meat. The bear lollops toward the herd.

The musk oxen run for it, but the drifts are deep and they sink into the snow. If they can't flee, they have to fight. The adults wheel, forming a ring around last year's young. The bear halts before the wall of horns, looking for an opening. Then one musk ox, a bull weighing almost as much as the bear, breaks formation to charge. The grizzly bolts: he'll search elsewhere for a meal.

Danger passed, the musk oxen regain their calm. The young oxen, and the calves about to be born, are safe. The long night is nearly over. Light — and life — will soon return to the Arctic.

ANTARCTICA

MARCH. Many miles from open ocean, mountains stand encased in ice. Only the highest peaks rise above the glaciers, their tips dusted with seabirds. Petrels have nested here for 30 000 years, and this year's chicks are about to fledge.

One petrel chick sits in her nest, alone and unguarded. But the south polar skua has a baby to feed — and this little bird would fit the bill. The skua strikes, but the chick doesn't flinch or flee. She shakes, she screams, she spits a yellow oil that smells like every rotten fish in the sea. The skua flaps wildly, avoiding the deadly stream, and flies away.

There's a dribble of oil on the chick's breast. It could damage her new adult feathers, which she needs to stay warm on cold waves. Leaving the nest, she bathes in the snow until the oil is gone. Then she spreads her wings, catches a mountain breeze … and turns toward a new life on the sea.

CLIMATE CHANGE AND THE POLAR REGIONS

Carbon dioxide is a greenhouse gas in the Earth's atmosphere that traps the sun's heat. The amount of carbon dioxide in the air has risen steadily since the nineteenth century and is now at its highest levels in 800 000 years. As a result, global temperatures are also rising: 2020 was one of the hottest years on record. But the planet is not warming evenly. The polar regions are heating up five times faster than anywhere else on Earth.

As a result, polar habitats are changing dramatically. Snow covers the Arctic for fewer days each decade, and the glaciers over Greenland and Antarctica are melting away. Sea ice is changing, too, getting thinner and covering less ocean. Polar bears depend on Arctic summer sea ice for hunting and traveling, but within a few decades, there might be none left.

Changes in climate and habitat have other consequences for polar animals. Some adaptations that supported survival are becoming unhelpful or even harmful. For example, blubber keeps marine mammals warm in cold water (see page 13). As temperatures continue to rise, the same blubber could cause those animals to overheat. When days get longer, ptarmigan turn brown for camouflage when the snow melts (see page 20). If warmer spring temperatures melt snow before the days lengthen, birds that are still white will be more visible to predators. As climate change continues, these and other polar species may find it harder to persist.

POLAR POLLUTION

Climate change is a major threat to polar ecosystems, but it's not the only one. From lead particles used in Ancient Roman water pipes, to refrigerator chemicals that punctured the ozone layer, humans have been polluting these remote and delicate habitats for thousands of years, sometimes without even being there.

Plastic pollution is a more recent problem. Global oceans contain more than 250 million t (276 million tn.) of plastic waste. More than 200 species of fish, mammals, turtles and seabirds eat this plastic. Recently, scientists identified one reason for this strange behavior. Ocean algae grows on floating plastic — the same algae that make distress signals to call hungry seabirds (see page 37). An adaptation that once led birds to fishing grounds now tells them that plastic is food ... and that mistake can be fatal.

HOW POLAR REGIONS AFFECT OUR WORLD

Global climate change alters the polar regions, but changes in the polar regions alter the entire globe. This is because of two cycles that speed up climate change.

The first cycle is known as the Ice-Albedo Feedback. Snow and ice have high albedos: they reflect sunlight and its heat, helping to keep the Earth cool. Bare tundra and dark oceans, however, have low albedos and absorb much more of the sun's heat. This heat melts surrounding snow and ice, revealing more tundra and ocean, which absorb more heat. Since 1979, changes in the Earth's albedo due to melting Arctic sea ice have caused 25 percent as much global warming as increased carbon dioxide in the atmosphere has caused.

The second cycle that's speeding up climate change is called the Permafrost Feedback. Greenhouse gases released into Earth's atmosphere are the leading cause of global warming. But not all greenhouse gases have an equal effect on climate. Methane has 23 times the warming power of carbon dioxide, and huge amounts of methane are locked in frozen permafrost ... or at least, they were. On the tundra, permafrost is melting due to warmer summer air; in shallow coastal areas, warmer water is melting permafrost under the seabed. As permafrost melts, bubbles of methane are released into the atmosphere. As methane levels in the atmosphere increase, so will the pace of climate change, causing even more permafrost to melt.

As they go, both of these cycles are getting bigger, faster and harder to stop — like snowballs rolling downhill. Both will have global consequences for years to come.

TAKE ACTION

There are many things you can do to help protect the polar regions from climate change. Here are some simple ways to take action today.

- Speak out:
  - Teach your friends and family about climate change.
  - Write letters to companies and politicians asking them to support climate-friendly policies.
  - Attend local climate protests with your friends and family.

- Reduce greenhouse gas emissions that come from burning fossil fuels:
  - Walk, bike or take public transit.
  - Reuse or recycle items, reducing emissions needed to produce and ship new products.
  - At the grocery store, choose foods that are in season and grown or made locally, reducing the distance the food has to travel.
  - Eat that food before it goes bad!

TO LEARN MORE

To learn more about saving polar animals and their habitats, visit:

National Geographic Kids: Save Our Polar Habitats!
www.natgeokids.com/uk/home-is-good/save-our-polar-habitats

Polar Bears International
www.polarbearsinternational.org/education-center/just-for-kids

GLOSSARY

adaptation: a body part, body function or behavior that helps a plant or animal survive in its environment

albedo: a measure of the amount of sunlight that reflects off a surface, where light-colored surfaces reflect more sunlight than dark ones

algae: small or large plants that grow in fresh water or seawater

Antarctica: a southern area of the planet that is bordered by the Antarctic Circumpolar Current

Antarctic Circle: an imaginary line encircling the bottom of the world with the South Pole at its center

Antarctic Circumpolar Current: a strong ocean current that encircles Antarctica, keeping the cold Southern Ocean isolated from warmer oceans to the north

Arctic: a northern area of the planet where the land is too cold and dry for trees to grow

Arctic Circle: an imaginary line encircling the top of the world with the North Pole at its center

axis: the imaginary line through the center of the Earth, between the North and South Poles, that the planet rotates around each day

blubber: a layer of body fat that helps whales and seals stay warm in cold oceans

camouflage: a means of blending into the surrounding environment using colors or patterns. Animals use camouflage to hide from predators or prey.

carbon dioxide: a greenhouse gas in the Earth's atmosphere that traps the sun's heat and contributes to climate change

circadian rhythm: an internal "clock" that tells animals the best time of day or night to eat, sleep or move throughout their habitats

cold-blooded: having a body temperature that is controlled by the temperature of the environment

ecosystem: a community of living things interacting with their natural environment

equator: an imaginary circle around the middle of the Earth, halfway between the North and South Poles

fledge: to grow adult feathers needed for flight and leave the nest for the first time

habitat: the type of place where an animal normally lives

larvae: young, wormlike forms of insects

mate (*n.*): one animal in a breeding pair

mate (*v.*): coming together to breed

midnight sun: daylight in the polar regions that lasts at least 24 hours in a row

migration: moving from one part of the world to another, often as seasons change, to avoid bad weather or find food or mates

mutualism: a partnership between animals of different species that benefits them all

North Pole: the most northern place on the Earth, and the northern end of the Earth's axis

northern lights: moving, colored lights that sometimes appear in the sky over the Arctic at night, also called the aurora borealis

orbit: the path that the Earth follows around the sun each year

polar night: night in the polar regions that lasts at least 24 hours in a row

predator: an animal that survives by hunting and eating other animals

prey: an animal that is hunted by another animal for food

South Pole: the most southern place on the Earth, and the southern end of the Earth's axis

southern lights: moving, colored lights that sometimes appear in the sky over Antarctica at night, also called the aurora australis

Southern Ocean: a small, cold ocean surrounding the continent and islands of Antarctica

swarm: a large number of animals of the same species grouped and moving together

synchronized: happening at the same time

tundra: northern habitats that are too cold and dry for trees to grow

warm-blooded: able to make body heat and keep a constant body temperature that's separate from the temperature of the environment

RESOURCES

FURTHER READING

Buller, Laura, Andrea Mills, and John Woodward. *Ice: Chilling Stories from a Disappearing World*. New York: DK, 2019.
Gifford, Clive. *In Focus: Polar Lands.* New York: Kingfisher, 2017.
Patkau, Karen. *Who Needs an Iceberg?* Toronto: Tundra Books, 2012.
Pelletier, Mia, and Danny Christopher. *A Children's Guide to Arctic Birds.* Toronto: Inhabit Media, 2014.
Spilsbury, Louise. *Research on the Edge: Polar Regions.* Mankato, MN: Smart Apple Media, 2016.
Strauss, Rochelle, and Natasha Donovan. *The Global Ocean.* Toronto: Kids Can Press, 2022.

SELECTED SOURCES

I consulted almost 350 sources while researching this book. When I couldn't find answers in papers by polar scientists, I asked the scientists themselves. In some cases, they didn't have the answers either! Polar research is difficult and expensive, and the ecosystems are changing quickly: where definitive information was unavailable, I made cautious educated guesses. Thank you to Dr. Eva Fuglei of the Norwegian Polar Institute and Dr. Nicholas Teets, Antarctic researcher with the University of Kentucky, for reviewing the manuscript and assuring me that it's correct to the best of our current knowledge.

BOOKS

Crawford, Robert M. M. *Tundra-Taiga Biology: Human, Plant, and Animal Survival in the Arctic.* Oxford: Oxford University Press, 2013.
Macdonald, David, ed. *The New Encyclopedia of Mammals.* Oxford: Oxford University Press, 2001.
Wadhams, Peter. *A Farewell to Ice: A Report from the Arctic.* London, UK: Allen Lane, 2016.
Walton, David W. H., ed. *Antarctica: Global Science from a Frozen Continent.* New York: Cambridge University Press, 2013.

ARTICLES

Ancel, André, Caroline Gilbert, Nicolas Poulin, Michaël Beaulieu, and Bernard Thierry. "New Insights into the Huddling Dynamics of Emperor Penguins." *Animal Behaviour* 110 (December 2015): 91–98.
Aubin, Thierry, Pierre Jouventin, and Isabelle Charrier. "Mother Vocal Recognition in Antarctic Fur Seal *Arctocephalus gazella* Pups: A Two-Step Process." *PLoS ONE* 10, no. 9 (2015).
Blix, Arnoldus Schytte. "Adaptations to Polar Life in Mammals and Birds." *Journal of Experimental Biology* 219, no. 8 (April 2016): 1093–1105.
Claes, Julien M., Dag L. Aksnes, and Jérôme Mallefet. "Phantom Hunter of the Fjords: Camouflage by Counterillumination in a Shark (*Etmopterus spinax*)." *Journal of Experimental Marine Biology and Ecology* 388, no. 1–2 (2010): 28–32.
Hauser, Donna D. W. "Seasonal Sea Ice and Arctic Migrations of the Beluga Whale." *Alaska Park Science* 17, no. 1 (2018). Migration: On the Move in Alaska. National Park Service. Accessed May 28, 2019. https://www.nps.gov/articles/aps-17-1-9.htm.
Piccolin, Fabio, Bettina Meyer, Alberto Biscontin, Cristiano De Pittà, So Kawaguchi, and Mathias Teschke. "Photoperiodic Modulation of Circadian Functions in Antarctic Krill *Euphausia superba* Dana, 1850 (Euphausiacea)." *Journal of Crustacean Biology* 38, no. 6 (November 2018): 707–715.
Rosvold, Jørgen. "Perennial Ice and Snow-Covered Land as Important Ecosystems for Birds and Mammals." *Journal of Biogeography* 43, no. 1 (January 2016): 3–12.
Savoca, Matthew S., and Gabrielle A. Nevitt. "Evidence That Dimethyl Sulfide Facilitates a Tritrophic Mutualism between Marine Primary Producers and Top Predators." *Proceedings of the National Academy of Sciences* 111, no. 11 (2014): 4157–4161.
Teets, Nicholas M., Yuta Kawarasaki, Leslie J. Potts, Benjamin N. Philip, J. D. Gantz, David L. Denlinger, and Richard E. Lee Jr. "Rapid Cold Hardening Protects against Sublethal Freezing Injury in an Antarctic Insect." *Journal of Experimental Biology* 222, no. 15 (Aug 2019): jeb206011.
Warham, John. "The Incidence, Functions and Ecological Significance of Petrel Stomach Oils." *Proceedings of the New Zealand Ecological Society* 24 (1977): 84–93.

INDEX

A

adaptations, 5
    behavioral, 19, 20, 26, 28, 32, 34, 38, 43
    physical, 10, 16, 20, 28, 32, 33, 34, 42
Alaska, 12
albedo, 18, 44
algae, 15, 31, 37, 43
Antarctic Circle, 6, 7
Antarctic Circumpolar Current, 6
Antarctica, 5
    climate, 19
    location, 6
    seasons, 18
antifreeze, 5, 16, 17
Arctic, 5
    climate, 19
    location, 6
    seasons, 18
Arctic Circle, 6, 7

B

Baffin Bay, 32
belugas, 12
Bering Sea, 12
Bransfield Strait, 15
breeding, 24–25, 27, 32

C

camouflage, 20–21, 42
Canada, 12, 32
caterpillars, 16, 22
circadian rhythm, 14–15
climate change, 42–43, 44–45
cod, 12, 29
communication, 32–33, 36

E

echolocation, 32
ermines, 30

F

feathers, 10, 11, 20, 24, 27, 39
food, 5, 10, 14, 22, 24, 26, 28, 29, 31, 36, 38
food webs, 31
foxes, 10, 20, 26
fur, 10

G

greenhouse gases, 42, 44, 45
Greenland, 32, 42
grizzly bears, 38
gulls, 24, 31

H

habitats, 5, 6, 14, 16, 30, 42, 43, 45
hares, 34
hibernation, 28, 29
huddling (for warmth), 26–27

I

Ice Age, 5
Ice-Albedo Feedback, 44

K

krill, 12, 15, 21, 31, 33, 35, 37

L

lemmings, 26, 30
lynx, 34

M

Mackenzie River Delta (Canada), 12
midges, 17
midnight sun, 7, 14, 16, 17, 37
migration, 5, 12–13, 19, 22, 27, 30
musk oxen, 38
mutualism, 36–37

N

narwhals, 32
New Zealand, 23
North Pole, 6, 7, 10

P

penguins, 25, 27, 35
permafrost, 30, 44
Permafrost Feedback, 44
petrels, 37, 39
plastic (in the ocean), 43
polar bears, 10, 42
polar night, 7, 14–15, 17, 32

pollution, 43
predators, protection from, 12, 15, 20–21, 24–25, 31, 32, 36–37, 38–39, 42
prions, 37
ptarmigan, 20, 42
puffins, 24

R

ravens, 36
reindeer, 14, 34, 36
Ross Sea, 23
Russia, 12, 26

S

seals, 23, 29, 31, 33
seasons, 18, 19
sharks, 21
shelter, 16–17, 26, 28–29
skuas, 11, 25, 39
snow and ice (as habitat), 30–31
snow buntings, 22
South Pole, 6, 7, 11
Southern Ocean, 6, 13, 29
squids, 13, 21
squirrels, 28
Svalbard (Norway), 14

T

terns, 19
traveling (over snow and ice), 10, 34–35
tundra, 6, 14, 16, 20, 34, 44

W

whales, 12–13, 31, 32
wolverines, 30
wolves, 36
Wrangel Island (Russia), 26